VAMPIRE WEE
CONTRA

Produced by
Alfred Music Publishing Co., Inc.
P.O. Box 10003
Van Nuys, CA 91410-0003
alfred.com

Printed in USA.

ISBN-10: 0-7390-6979-9
ISBN-13: 978-0-7390-6979-0

Cover photograph by Tod Brody, Band photograph by Chris Tomson
Design by Rostam Batmanglij & Asher Sarlin

 Alfred Cares. Contents printed on 100% recycled paper.

C000157106

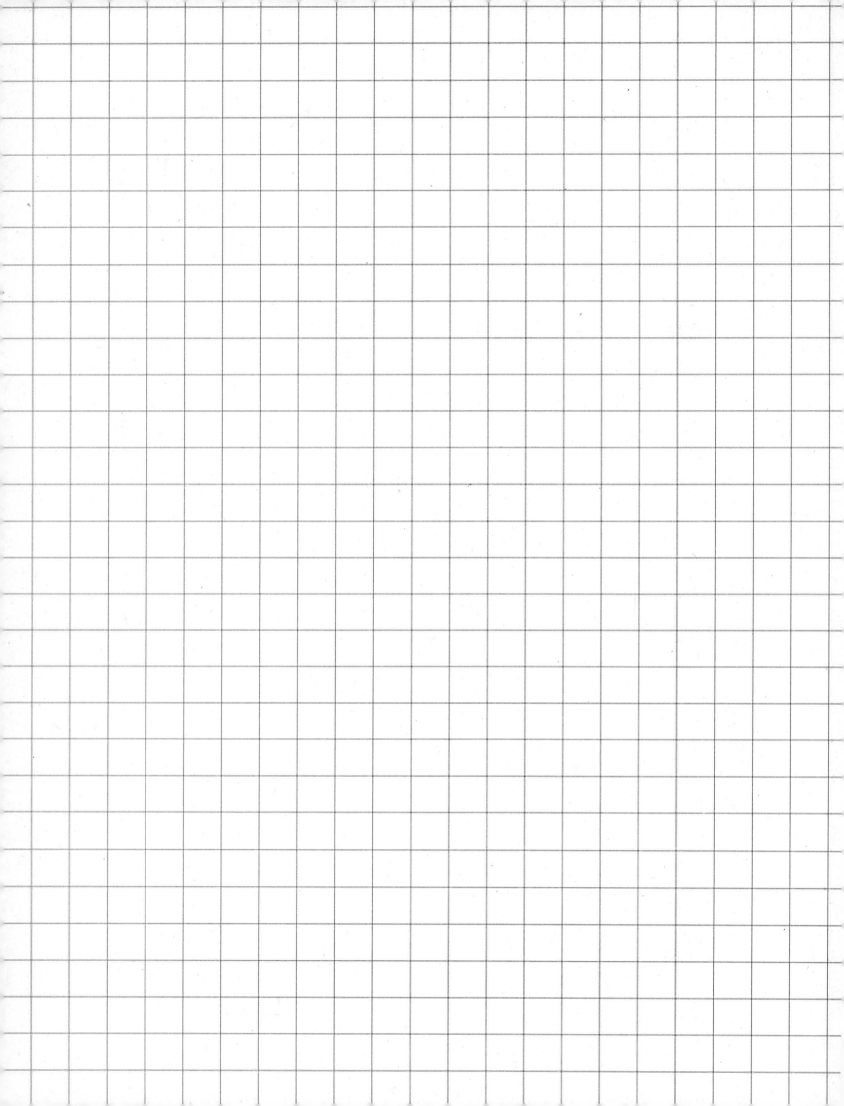

CONTENTS

HORCHATA

IN DECEMBER, DRINKING HORCHATA
I'D LOOK PSYCHOTIC IN A BALACLAVA
WINTER'S COLD IS TOO MUCH TO HANDLE
PINCHER CRABS THAT PINCH AT YOUR SANDALS

IN DECEMBER, DRINKING HORCHATA
LOOK DOWN YOUR GLASSES AT THAT ARANCIATA
WITH LIPS AND TEETH TO ASK HOW MY DAY WENT
BOOTS AND FISTS TO POUND ON THE PAVEMENT

HERE COMES A FEELING YOU THOUGHT YOU'D FORGOTTEN
CHAIRS TO SIT AND SIDEWALKS TO WALK ON

YOU'D REMEMBER DRINKING HORCHATA
YOU'D STILL ENJOY IT WITH YOUR FOOT ON MASADA

WINTER'S COLD IS TOO MUCH TO HANDLE
PINCHER CRABS THAT PINCH AT YOUR SANDALS

HERE COMES A FEELING YOU THOUGHT YOU'D FORGOTTEN
CHAIRS TO SIT AND SIDEWALKS TO WALK ON
OH YOU HAD IT BUT OH NO YOU LOST IT
LOOKING BACK YOU SHOULDN'T HAVE FOUGHT IT

IN DECEMBER, DRINKING HORCHATA
I'D LOOK PSYCHOTIC IN A BALACLAVA
BUT WINTER'S COLD IS 2 MUCH 2 HANDLE
PINCHER CRABS THAT PINCH AT YOUR SANDALS
YEARS GO BY AND HEARTS START TO HARDEN
THOSE PALMS AND FIRS THAT GREW IN YOUR GARDEN
ARE FALLING DOWN AND NEARING THE ROSEBEDS
THE ROOTS ARE SHOOTING UP THROUGH THE TOOL SHED
THOSE LIPS AND TEETH THAT ASKED HOW MY DAY WENT
ARE SHOUTING UP THROUGH CRACKS IN THE PAVEMENT

HERE COMES A FEELING YOU THOUGHT YOU'D FORGOTTEN
CHAIRS TO SIT AND SIDEWALKS TO WALK ON
OH YOU HAD IT BUT OH NO YOU LOST IT
YOU UNDERSTOOD SO YOU SHOULDN'T HAVE FOUGHT IT

WHITE SKY

AN ANCIENT BUSINESS
A MODERN PIECE OF GLASSWORK
DOWN ON THE CORNER THAT YOU WALK EACH DAY IN PASSING

THE ELDERLY SALES CLERK WON'T EYE US WITH SUSPICION
THE WHOLE, IMMORTAL CORPORATION'S GIVEN ITS PERMISSION

A LITTLE STAIRWAY
A LITTLE PIECE OF CARPET
A PAIR OF MIRRORS THAT ARE FACING ONE ANOTHER

OUT IN BOTH DIRECTIONS, A THOUSAND LITTLE JULIA'S
THAT COME TOGETHER IN THE MIDDLE OF MANHATTAN

YOU WAITED SINCE LUNCH
IT ALL COMES AT ONCE

CHORUS

AROUND THE CORNER, THE HOUSE THAT MODERN ART BUILT
A HOUSE FOR MODERN ART TO KEEP IT OUT THE CLOSETS
OF PEOPLE WHO MIGHT OWN IT
THE SINS OF PRIDE AND ENVY
AND ON THE SECOND FLOOR, THE RICHARD SERRA SKATEPARK

YOU WAITED SINCE LUNCH
IT ALL COMES AT ONCE

CHORUS

SIT ON THE PARK WALL
ASK ALL THE RIGHT QUESTIONS
"WHY ARE THE HORSES RACING TAXIS IN THE WINTER?"

LOOK UP AT THE BUILDINGS
IMAGINE WHO MIGHT LIVE THERE
IMAGINING YOUR WOLFORDS IN A BALL UPON THE SINK THERE

YOU WAITED SINCE LUNCH
IT ALL COMES AT ONCE

CHORUS

HOLIDAY

HOLIDAY, O, A HOLIDAY!
AND THE BEST ONE OF THE YEAR
DOZING OFF UNDERNEATH MY SHEETS
WHILE I COVER BOTH MY EARS

BUT IF I WAIT FOR A HOLIDAY COULD IT STOP MY FEAR?
TO GO AWAY ON A SUMMER'S DAY NEVER SEEMED SO CLEAR

HOLIDAY, STILL SO FAR AWAY
OUR REPUBLIC ON THE BEACH
I CAN'T FORGET JUST HOW BAD IT GETS
WHEN I'M COUNTING ON MY TEETH

BUT IF I WAIT FOR A HOLIDAY
COULD IT STOP MY FEAR?
TO GO AWAY ON A SUMMER'S DAY
NEVER SEEMED SO CLEAR

A VEGETARIAN SINCE THE INVASION
SHE'D NEVER SEEN THE WORD BOMBS
SHE'D NEVER SEEN THE WORD BOMBS BLOWN UP
TO 96 POINT FUTURA
SHE'D NEVER SEEN AN AK
IN A YELLOWY DAY-GLO DISPLAY
A T-SHIRT SO LOVELY IT TURNED ALL THE HISTORY BOOKS GREY

I'VE GOT WHEELS, I'VE GOT CUTTER SPRAY
AND A HEALTHY SENSE OF WORTH
HALF OF ME IS THE GASOLINE
BUT THE OTHER HALF'S THE SURF

SO IF I WAIT FOR A HOLIDAY COULD IT STOP MY FEAR?
TO GO AWAY ON A SUMMER'S DAY NEVER SEEMED SO CLEAR

CALIFORNIA ENGLISH

WOULDN'T EVER GAG YOU WITH A SPOON, MY ONLY TRUE LOVE
NEVER REALLY HEARD YOU SPEAK THAT WAY, IT'S UNWORTHY OF...
FUNNY HOW THAT LITTLE COLLEGE GIRL CALLED LANGUAGE CORRUPT
FUNNY HOW THE OTHER PRIVATE SCHOOLS HAD NO HAPA CLUB

SOMEONE TOOK A TRIP BEFORE YOU CAME TO SKI IN THE ALPS
YOUR FATHER MOVED ACROSS THE COUNTRY
JUST TO SUNBURN HIS SCALP
CONTRA COSTA, CONTRA MUNDUM, CONTRADICT WHAT I SAY
LIVING LIKE THE FRENCH CONNECTION, BUT WE'LL DIE IN LA

BLASTED FROM A DISCONNECTED LIGHT SWITCH
THROUGH THE CONDO THAT THEY'LL NEVER FINISH
BOUNCED ACROSS A SAUDI SATELLITE DISH
AND THROUGH YOUR BRAIN TO CALIFORNIA ENGLISH

NO ONE SITS INSIDE A FREEZING FLAT AND STAYS THERE TIL MAY
LEAFING THROUGH A STACK OF A-Z'S TO SURF THE UK
WAITING WITH THE WIND AGAINST YOUR FACE
AND GEL IN YOUR HAIR
SHIVERING IN LITTLE UNDERSHIRTS, BUT DON'T SEEM TO CARE

BLASTED FROM A DISCONNECTED LIGHT SWITCH
THROUGH THE CONDO THAT THEY'LL NEVER FINISH
BOUNCED ACROSS A SAUDI SATELLITE DISH
AND THROUGH YOUR BRAIN TO CALIFORNIA ENGLISH

SWEET CAROB RICE CAKE
SHE DON'T CARE HOW THE SWEETS TASTE
FAKE PHILLY CHEESE STEAK
BUT SHE USE REAL TOOTHPASTE

CUZ IF THAT TOM'S DON'T WORK
IF IT JUST MAKES YOU WORSE
WOULD YOU LOSE ALL OF YOUR FAITH IN THE GOOD EARTH?

AND IF IT'S ALL A CURSE
AND WE'RE JUST GETTING WORSE
BABY, PLEASE DON'T LOSE YOUR FAITH IN THE GOOD EARTH

BLASTED FROM A DISCONNECTED LIGHT SWITCH
THROUGH THE CONDO THAT THEY'LL NEVER FINISH
BOUNCED ACROSS A SAUDI SATELLITE DISH
AND THROUGH YOUR BRAIN TO CALIFORNIA ENGLISH

TAXI CAB

UNSENTIMENTAL
TRAVELING AROUND
SURE OF MYSELF
SURE OF IT NOW

BUT YOU WERE STANDING THERE SO CLOSE TO ME
LIKE THE FUTURE WAS SUPPOSED TO BE
IN THE AISLES OF THE GROCERY
AND THE BLOCKS UPTOWN

I REMEMBER
REMEMBER WELL
BUT IF I'D FORGOTTEN
COULD YOU TELL?

IN THE SHADOW OF YOUR FIRST ATTACK,
I WAS QUESTIONING AND LOOKING BACK
YOU SAID, "BABY, WE DON'T SPEAK OF THAT"
LIKE A REAL ARISTOCRAT

COMPOUND TO COMPOUND
LAZY AND SAFE
WANTED TO LEAVE IT
WANTED TO WAIT

WHEN THE TAXI DOOR WAS OPEN WIDE,
I PRETENDED I WAS HORRIFIED

BY THE UNIFORM AND GLOVES OUTSIDE
OF THE COURTYARD GATE

YOU'RE NOT A VICTIM
BUT NEITHER AM I
NOSTALGIC FOR GARBAGE
DESPERATE FOR TIME

I COULD BLAME IT ON YOUR MOTHER'S HAIR
OR THE COLORS THAT YOUR FATHER WEARS
BUT I KNOW THAT I WAS NEVER FAIR
YOU WERE ALWAYS FINE

RUN

EVERY DOLLAR COUNTS
AND EVERY MORNING HURTS
WE MOSTLY WORK TO LIVE
UNTIL WE LIVE TO WORK

SHE SAID,
"YOU KNOW
THERE'S NOWHERE ELSE TO GO"
BUT CHANGING ROLES
IT STRUCK ME THAT THE TWO OF US COULD RUN

WORLDS AWAY FROM CARS
AND ALL THE STARS AND BARS
WHERE A LITTLE BIT OF CONDENSATION MEANS SO MUCH
AND A LITTLE BIT OF CHANGE IS ALL YOUR LITTLE FINGERS TOUCH

I SAID,
"YOU KNOW
THERE'S NOWHERE ELSE TO GO"
BUT CHANGING ROLES
IT STRUCK ME THAT THE TWO OF US COULD RUN

HONEY, WITH YOU
IS THE ONLY HONEST WAY TO GO
AND I COULD TAKE TWO
BUT I REALLY COULDN'T EVER KNOW

HONEY, WITH YOU
AND A BATTERED RADIO

WE COULD TRY

SO LEAD MY FEET AWAY
CUZ ALL THEY'LL DO IS STAY
AND I DON'T THINK YOUR EYES
HAVE EVER LOOKED SURPRISED

SHE SAID,
"YOU KNOW
THERE'S NOWHERE LEFT TO GO"
BUT WITH HER FUND
IT STRUCK ME THAT THE TWO OF US COULD RUN

HONEY, WITH YOU
IS THE ONLY HONEST WAY TO GO
AND I COULD TAKE TWO
BUT I REALLY COULDN'T EVER KNOW

HONEY, WITH YOU
AND A BATTIN RADIO

WE COULD TRY

COUSINS

YOU FOUND A SWEATER ON THE OCEAN FLOOR
THEY'RE GONNA FIND IT IF YOU DIDN'T CLOSE THE DOOR
YOU AND THE SMART ONES SIT OUTSIDE OF THEIR SIGHT
IN A HOUSE ON A STREET THEY WOULDN'T PARK ON AT NIGHT

DAD WAS A RISK-TAKER
HIS WAS A SHOEMAKER
YOU, GREATEST HITS 2006 LITTLE LIST-MAKER,
HEARD CODES IN THE MELODIES
YOU HEEDED THE CALL
YOU WERE BORN WITH TEN FINGERS
AND YOU'RE GONNA USE EM ALL

INTERESTING COLORS I DISCOVERED MYSELF
IF YOUR ART LIFE IS GRITTY, YOU'LL BE TOASTING MY HEALTH
IF AN INTEREST IN CULTURE SHOULD BE LINING THE WALL,
WHEN YOUR BIRTHRIGHT IS INTEREST YOU COULD JUST ACCRUE IT ALL

ME AND MY COUSINS AND
YOU AND YOUR COUSINS
IT'S A LINE THAT'S ALWAYS RUNNING

ME AND MY COUSINS AND
YOU AND YOUR COUSINS
I CAN FEEL IT COMING

YOU COULD TURN YOUR BACK ON THE BITTER WORLD

GIVING UP THE GUN

YOUR SWORD'S GROWN OLD AND RUSTY
BURNT BENEATH THE RISING SUN
IT'S LOCKED UP LIKE A TROPHY
FORGETTING ALL THE THINGS IT'S DONE

AND THOUGH IT'S BEEN A LONG TIME
YOU'RE RIGHT BACK WHERE YOU STARTED FROM
I SEE IT IN YOUR EYES
THAT NOW YOU'RE GIVING UP THE GUN

WHEN I WAS 17
I HAD WRISTS LIKE STEEL
AND I FELT COMPLETE

AND NOW MY BODY FADES
BEHIND A BRASS CHARADE
AND I'M OBSOLETE

BUT IF THE CHANCE REMAINED
TO SEE THOSE BETTER DAYS
I'D CUT THE CANNONS DOWN

MY EARS ARE BLOWN TO BITS
FROM ALL THE RIFLE HITS
BUT STILL I CRAVE THAT SOUND

CHORUS

I HEARD YOU PLAY GUITAR
DOWN AT A SEEDY BAR
WHERE SKINHEADS USED TO FIGHT

YOUR TOKUGAWA SMILE
AND YOUR GARBAGE STYLE
USED TO SAVE THE NIGHT

YOU FELT THE COMING WAVE
TOLD ME WE'D ALL BE BRAVE
YOU SAID YOU WOULDN'T FLINCH

BUT IN THE YEARS THAT PASSED
SINCE I SAW YOU LAST
YOU HAVEN'T MOVED AN INCH

CHORUS

I SEE YOU SHINE IN YOUR WAY
GO ON, GO ON, GO ON

CHORUS

DIPLOMAT'S SON

IT'S NOT RIGHT BUT IT'S NOW OR NEVER
AND IF I WAIT COULD I EVER FORGIVE MYSELF?

ON A NIGHT WHEN THE MOON GLOWS YELLOW IN THE RIPTIDE
WITH THE LIGHT FROM THE TV'S BUZZING IN THE HOUSE

CUZ I'M GONNA CUT IT WHERE I CAN
AND THEN I'M GONNA DUCK OUT BEHIND THEM
IF I EVER HAD A CHANCE IT'S NOW THEN
BUT I NEVER HAD THE FEELING I COULD OFFER THAT TO YOU

TO OFFER IT TO YOU WOULD BE CRUEL
WHEN ALL I WANT TO DO IS USE, USE YOU

HE WAS A DIPLOMAT'S SON
IT WAS '81

DRESSED IN WHITE WITH MY CAR KEYS HIDDEN IN THE KITCHEN
I COULD SLEEP WHEREVER I LAY MY HEAD

AND THE SIGHT OF YOUR TWO SHOES SITTING IN THE BATHTUB
LET ME KNOW THAT I SHOULDN'T GIVE UP JUST YET

CUZ I'M GONNA TAKE IT FROM SIMON
AND THEN I'M GONNA DUCK OUT BEHIND THEM
IF I EVER HAD A CHANCE IT'S NOW THEN
BUT I NEVER HAD THE FEELING I COULD OFFER THAT TO YOU

TO OFFER IT TO YOU WOULD BE CRUEL
WHEN ALL I WANT TO DO IS USE, USE YOU

HE WAS A DIPLOMAT'S SON
IT WAS '81

I KNOW, YOU'LL SAY
I'M NOT DOING IT RIGHT
BUT THIS IS HOW I WANT IT

I CAN'T GO BACK
TO HOW I FELT BEFORE
THERE'S—

THAT NIGHT I SMOKED A JOINT
WITH MY BEST FRIEND
WE FOUND OURSELVES IN BED
WHEN I WOKE UP HE WAS GONE

HE WAS THE DIPLOMAT'S SON
IT WAS '81

LOOKING OUT AT THE ICE-COLD WATER ALL AROUND ME
I CAN'T FEEL ANY TRACES OF THAT OTHER PLACE

IN THE DARK WHEN THE WIND COMES RACING OFF THE RIVER
THERE'S A CAR ALL BLACK WITH DIPLOMATIC PLATES

I THINK UR A CONTRA

I HAD A FEELING ONCE
THAT YOU AND I
COULD TELL EACH OTHER EVERYTHING
FOR TWO MONTHS

BUT EVEN WITH AN OATH
WITH TRUTH ON OUR SIDE
WHEN YOU TURN AWAY FROM ME
IT'S NOT RIGHT

I THINK UR A CONTRA

MY REVOLUTION THOUGHTS
YOUR LITTLE ARROWS OF DESIRE
I WANT TO TRACE THEM TO THE SOURCE
AND THE WIRE

BUT IT'S NOT USEFUL NOW
SINCE WE'VE BOTH MADE UP OUR MINDS
YOU'RE GOING TO WATCH OUT FOR YOURSELF
AND SO WILL I

I THINK UR A CONTRA
AND I THINK THAT YOU'VE LIED
DON'T CALL ME A CONTRA
TIL YOU'VE TRIED

YOU WANTED GOOD SCHOOLS AND FRIENDS WITH POOLS
YOU'RE NOT A CONTRA

YOU WANTED ROCK AND ROLL, COMPLETE CONTROL
WELL, I DON'T KNOW

NEVER PICK SIDES
NEVER CHOOSE BETWEEN TWO
WELL I JUST WANTED YOU
I JUST WANTED YOU

YOU SAID,
"NEVER PICK SIDES
NEVER CHOOSE BETWEEN TWO"
WELL I JUST WANTED YOU
I JUST WANTED YOU

I THINK UR A CONTRA
AND I THINK THAT YOU'VE LIED
DON'T CALL ME A CONTRA
TIL YOU'VE TRIED

HORCHATA

Lyrics by
ROSTAM BATMANGLIJ and EZRA KOENIG
Music by
CHRIS BAIO, ROSTAM BATMANGLIJ,
EZRA KOENIG and CHRISTOPHER TOMSON

Horchata - 5 - 1

Horchata - 5 - 2

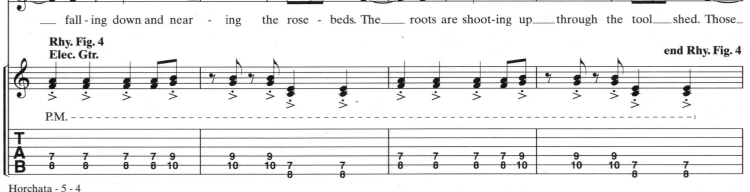

WHITE SKY

Lyrics by
EZRA KOENIG
Music by
CHRIS BAIO, ROSTAM BATMANGLIJ,
EZRA KOENIG and CHRISTOPHER TOMSON

White Sky - 4 - 1

HOLIDAY

Lyrics by
EZRA KOENIG
Music by
CHRIS BAIO, ROSTAM BATMANGLIJ,
EZRA KOENIG and CHRISTOPHER TOMSON

*Chord frames are suggested.

go a-way___ on a sum-mer's day___ nev-er seemed___ so clear.___

(1st time only) - |

(2nd & 3rd time only) - |

To Coda ⊕

Interlude:

Bridge:

A veg-e-tar - i-an since_ the in-va-sion, she'd nev-er seen_ the word bombs.

Rhy. Fig. 2
Elec. Gtr. 1

end Rhy. Fig. 2

Rhy. Fig. 2A
Elec. Gtr. 2

end Rhy. Fig. 2A

w/Rhy. Figs. 2 *(Elec. Gtr. 1)* **& 2A** *(Elec. Gtr. 2), both 2 times*

She'd nev-er seen_ the word bombs blown_ up to nine-ty-six point_ fu-tur-a.

She'd nev-er seen_ an A K in a yel-low-y day-glo dis-play. A

CALIFORNIA ENGLISH

Lyrics by
EZRA KOENIG
Music by
CHRIS BAIO, ROSTAM BATMANGLIJ,
EZRA KOENIG and CHRISTOPHER TOMSON

California English - 4 - 1

*Suggested strum pattern.

California English - 4 - 2

Instrumental:

*Suggested strum pattern.

Cont. rhy. simile
Rhy. Fig. 2
Elec. Gtr.

end Rhy. Fig. 2

P.M. -

w/Rhy. Fig. 2 *(Elec. Gtr.) 2 times, simile*

Oh   oh   oh   oh.   Oh   oh   oh   oh.

*Suggested strum pattern.

Cont. rhy. simile

Oh   oh   oh   oh.   Oh   oh   oh   oh.

Chorus:

w/Rhy. Fig. 1 *(Elec. Gtr.) 4 times*

Resume chorus fig. simile

Blast-ed from___ a dis-con-nect-ed light switch,   through the con-do

that they'll nev-er fin-ish.   Bounced a-cross___ a Sau-di sat-el-lite___ dish.

1.

2.

And through your brain___ to Cal-i-for-ni-a Eng-lish.   Cal-i-for-ni-a Eng-lish.

California English - 4 - 4

TAXI CAB

Lyrics by
EZRA KOENIG
Music by
ROSTAM BATMANGLIJ and EZRA KOENIG

*Suggested strum pattern.

moth - er's hair,___ or the col - ors that your fa - ther wears.___ But I know that I was

nev - er fair,___ you were al - ways___ fine.

Instrumental:

w/Rhy. Fig. 1 *(piano arr. for gtr.) simile*

1.2.3.

4.

*Suggested strum pattern.

Cont. rhy. simile

D.S. % al Coda

⊕ *Coda*

Outro:

*Suggested strum pattern.

ris - to - crat.___

Un - sen - ti -

w/Rhy. Fig. 1 *(piano arr. for gtr.) 2 times, simile*

Cont. rhy. simile

*Suggested strum pattern.

Taxi Cab - 4 - 4

RUN

Lyrics by
EZRA KOENIG

Music by
CHRIS BAIO, ROSTAM BATMANGLIJ,
EZRA KOENIG and CHRISTOPHER TOMSON

*Chords are implied.
Suggested strum pattern.

COUSINS

Lyrics by
EZRA KOENIG
Music by
CHRIS BAIO, ROSTAM BATMANGLIJ,
EZRA KOENIG and CHRISTOPHER TOMSON

*Chords are implied.
Suggested strum pattern.

40

GIVING UP THE GUN

Lyrics by
EZRA KOENIG
Music by
CHRIS BAIO, ROSTAM BATMANGLIJ,
EZRA KOENIG and CHRISTOPHER TOMSON

Moderately ♩ = 128

Intro:

Elec. Gtr. 1

*Chords are implied.
Suggested strum pattern.

Your sword's grown old and rust - y, burnt be - neath__ the ris - ing sun.__

Cont. rhy. simile

It's locked up like a tro - phy, for - get - ting all__ the things it's done.__

*Bass plays G♯.

And though it's been a long__ time, you're right back where you start - ed from.__

Giving Up the Gun - 5 - 1

*Lower set of chord frames, 1st time only.
 Higher set of chord frames, 2nd time only.
**Elec. Gtr. 2 w/Drop D, ⑥ = D.

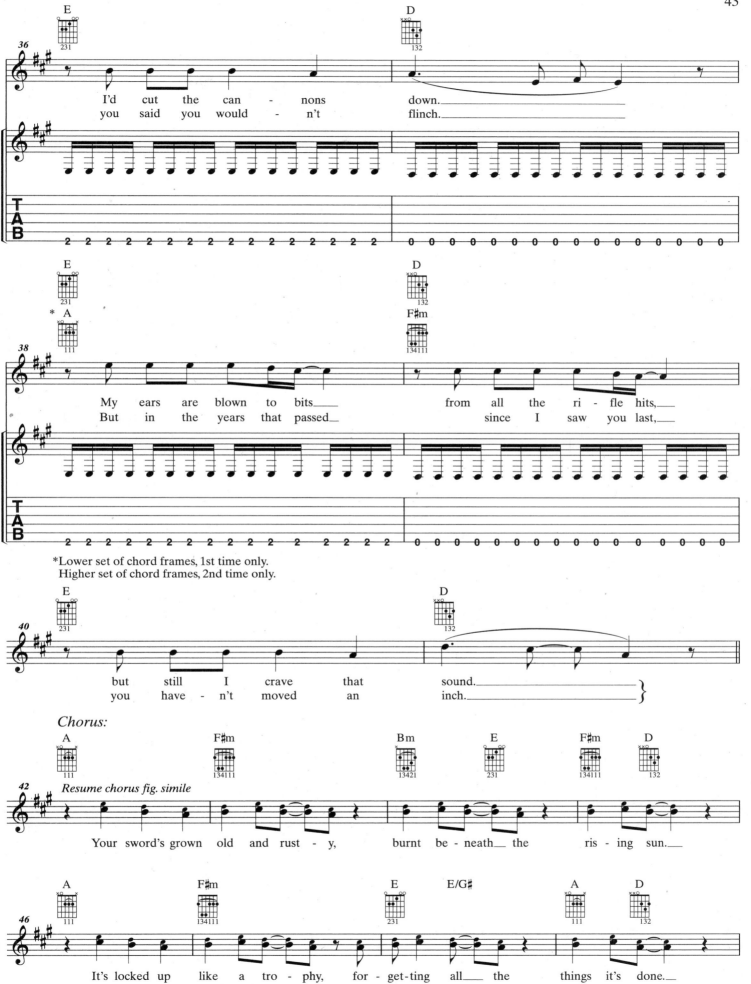

Giving Up the Gun - 5 - 3

44

DIPLOMAT'S SON

Lyrics by ROSTAM BATMANGLIJ and EZRA KOENIG
Music by CHRIS BAIO, ROSTAM BATMANGLIJ,
EZRA KOENIG, CHRISTOPHER TOMSON,
FREDERICK "TOOTS" HIBBERT, MATHANGI ARULPRAGASAM,
DAVE TAYLOR and THOMAS PENTZ

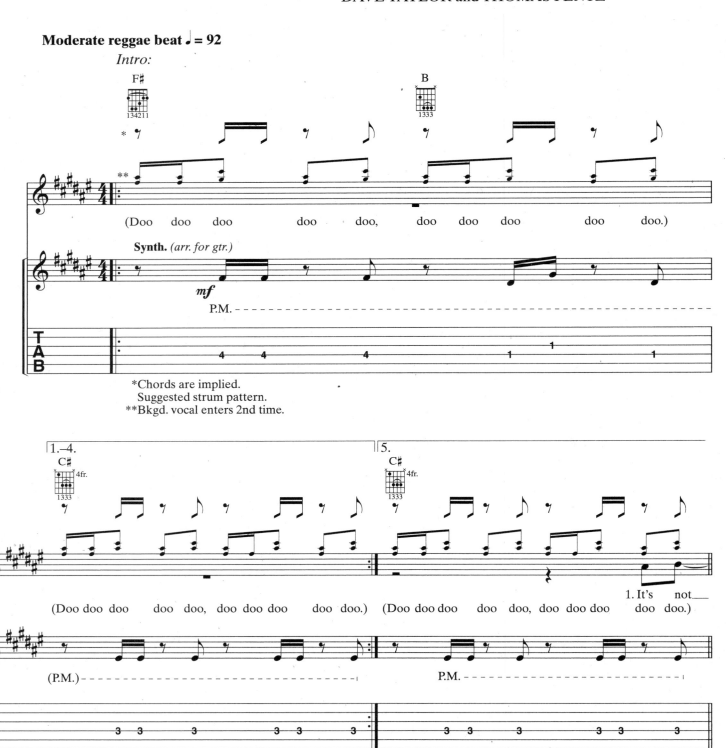

*Chords are implied.
 Suggested strum pattern.
**Bkgd. vocal enters 2nd time.

Diplomat's Son - 6 - 1

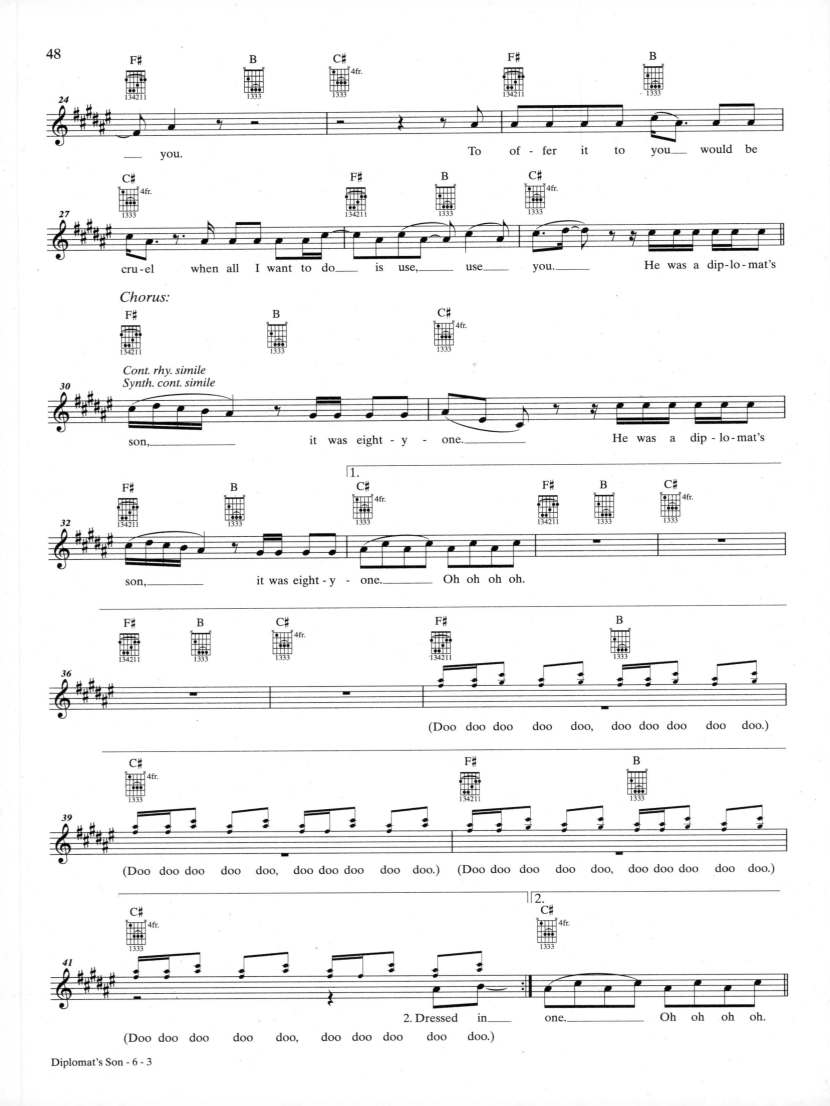

He was a dip - lo - mat's son,_____ it was eight - y - one._____

He was a dip - lo - mat's son,_____ it was eight - y - one._____

Verse 4:

Resume verse fig. simile
Synth. resume into fig. simile
Elec. Gtr. cont. simile

___ out   at the ice - cold wa - ter all a - round me.___

I can't___ feel___   an - y trac - es of that oth - er___

___place.   In the dark   when the wind comes rac - ing off the

riv - er,___   there's a   car___

___   all black with dip - lo - mat - ic___ plates.

I THINK UR A CONTRA

Lyrics by
EZRA KOENIG
Music by
ROSTAM BATMANGLIJ and EZRA KOENIG

Moderately slow ♩. = 92

Verse 3:

Never pick sides,___ nev - er choose be - tween two.___ But I

just want - ed you,___ I just want - ed you.___ You said,

"Nev - er pick sides,___ nev - er choose be - tween two."___ But I

TABLATURE EXPLANATION

TAB illustrates the six strings of the guitar.
Notes and chords are indicated by the placement of fret numbers on each string.

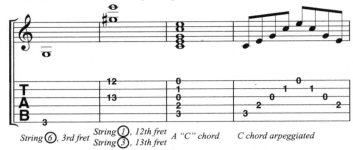

String ⑥, 3rd fret   String ①, 12th fret   A "C" chord   C chord arpeggiated
                String ③, 13th fret

BENDING NOTES

Half Step:
Play the note and bend string one half step (one fret).

Whole Step:
Play the note and bend string one whole step (two frets).

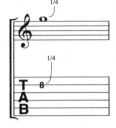

Slight Bend/ Quarter-Tone Bend:
Play the note and bend string sharp.

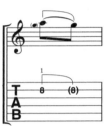

Prebend and Release:
Play the already-bent string, then immediately drop it down to the fretted note.

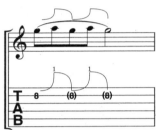

Bend and Release:
Play the note and bend to the next pitch, then release to the original note. Only the first note is attacked.

PICK DIRECTION

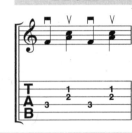

Downstrokes and Upstrokes:
The downstroke is indicated with this symbol (⊓) and the upstroke is indicated with this (∨).

ARTICULATIONS

Hammer On:
Play the lower note, then "hammer" your finger to the higher note. Only the first note is plucked.

Pull Off:
Play the higher note with your first finger already in position on the lower note. Pull your finger off the first note with a strong downward motion that plucks the string—sounding the lower note.

Palm Mute:
The notes are muted (muffled) by placing the palm of the pick hand lightly on the strings, just in front of the bridge.

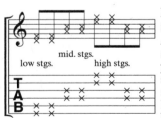

Muted Strings:
A percussive sound is produced by striking the strings while laying the fret hand across them.

Legato Slide:
Play the first note and, keeping pressure applied on the string, slide up to the second note. The diagonal line shows that it is a slide and not a hammer-on or a pull-off.

HARMONICS

Natural Harmonic:
A finger of the fret hand lightly touches the string at the note indicated in the TAB and is plucked by the pick producing a bell-like sound called a harmonic.

RHYTHM SLASHES

Strum Marks/ Rhythm Slashes:
Strum with the indicated rhythm pattern. Strum marks can be located above the staff or within the staff.

Single Notes with Rhythm Slashes:
Sometimes single notes are incorporated into a strum pattern. The circled number below is the string and the fret number is above.

Artificial Harmonic:
Fret the note at the first TAB number, lightly touch the string at the fret indicated in parens (usually 12 frets higher than the fretted note), then pluck the string with an available finger or your pick.